T0372573

CAMBRIDGE
Global English Starters

Fun with Letters and Sounds C

Gabrielle Pritchard

I am _____ .

This is my Fun with Letters and Sounds book.

Cambridge Global English Starters **Fun with Letters and Sounds C Review**

I can do it!

1 Point and say the letters.

Write the missing letters.

A			b	C			d	E	

	f	G			h	I			j

K			l	M			n	O	

	p	Q			r

2 Can you remember?

Say the sound. Write the letters to complete the words.

eaf

encil

ite

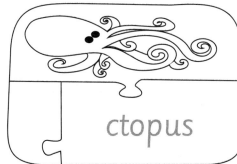

ctopus

ain

ine

uilt

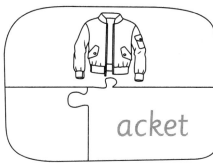

acket

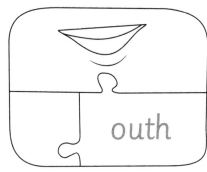

outh

3 Look at the pictures and say.

Choose and write the correct letter.

j   k   l   m   n   o

_ey   _live   _ion

_onkey   _ug   _et

4 Say and match the words with the same sound.

Cambridge Global English Starters **Fun with Letters and Sounds C Review**

5 **Look and complete the words with j, k, l, m, n or o.**
Then match.

_range   _ango   _ing   _uts   _ake   _ump

6 ⇕ **Join the dots.**
Read, count and write the number. Then complete.

This is an _ctopus.   It has got _ legs.

Unit 7

1 Let's learn our letters

 1 Listen and trace.

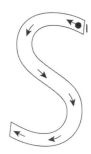  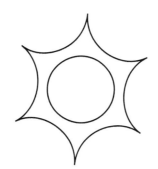 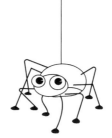 

 2a Listen, point and say.

 2b Listen, find and say.

3 Trace and write.

4 ▲▲ Write.

5 Complete the letter suns.

Write **S** and **s**.

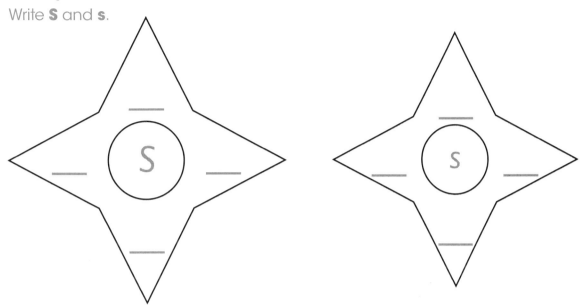

6 Circle the things that begin with **S**.

Point and say.

7 ▲▲ Read and colour the picture.

Write.

The _un is yellow.
The _piders are black.
The _ofas are orange.

2 Let's learn our letters

4 **1** Listen and trace.

5 **2a** Listen, point and say.

6 **2b** Listen, find and say.

3 Trace and write.

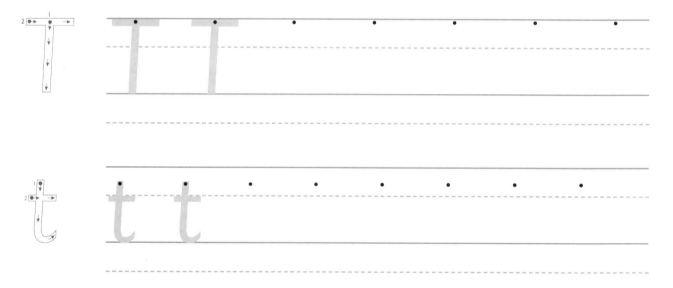

4 ▲▲ Write.

5 Find and trace S, s and T, t.
Use 2 colours.

s l s t c t l s t

T J S Z T S F T F

6 Say and write s or t.

_ing   _ree   _able   _mell

_pider   _iger   _oys   _ofa

7 ▲▲ Say the sounds and complete the pictures.
Then write.

s + u + n   t + a + p   t + e + n + t

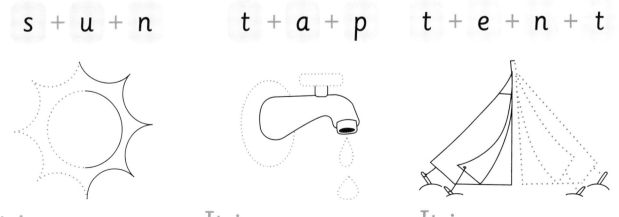

It is a _____ . It is a _____ . It is a _____ .

3 Let's learn our letters

 7 **1** Listen and trace.

 8 **2a** Listen, point and say.

 9 **2b** Listen, find and say.

3 Trace and write.

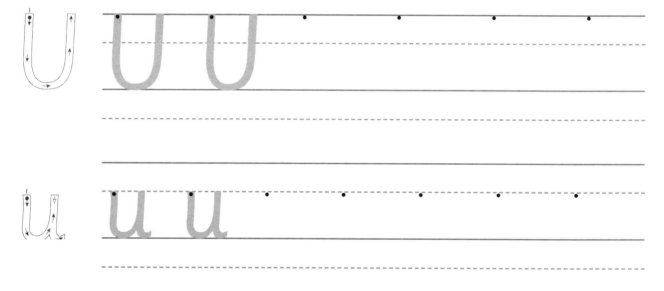

4 ▲▲ Write.

5 Find and trace S, s, T, t and U, u.

Use 3 colours. Then circle and match.

S g u U S T
S s U G e u
U S E t T t

6 Look at the pictures.

Complete the words. Use **s**, **t** or **u**. Then trace and say.

| _ | e | n | t |

| _ | n | d | e | r |

n
c
l

| _ | p | i | d | e | r |

o
f
a

7 ▲▲ **Look and write.**

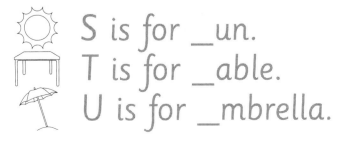

S is for _un.

T is for _able.

U is for _mbrella.

4 Story time: Tara and the spiders

 1 Listen and point.

 2 Listen, say and circle or write.

Tara sits on a sofa in a tent.

A spider sits under the table in the tent.

Tara sees the spider and screams.

Tara sits under an umbrella in the sun.

The spider sees his six uncles in a tree.

Now there are seven spiders under the umbrella!

3 Find and colour the letters.
What is the word? Write.

5 I can do it!

1 Listen, find and write.

uncle   tent   spider   table   under   tree   sun

There is a
_ _ _ _ _ _ on
the _ _ _ _ _ .

My _ _ _ _ _ is
in the _ _ _ .

The _ _ _ _ is
_ _ _ _ _ the
_ _ _ _ .

2 Draw lines to match the letters.

S   t   **u**   **t**

T   s   **S**   **U**

U   u   **T**   **s**

3 Write the missing letters.

Then match the pictures that start with the same sound.

 _ofa •

•  _oys

 _iger •

•  _nder

 _mbrella •

•  _ix

1 Let's learn our letters

13 **1** Listen and trace.

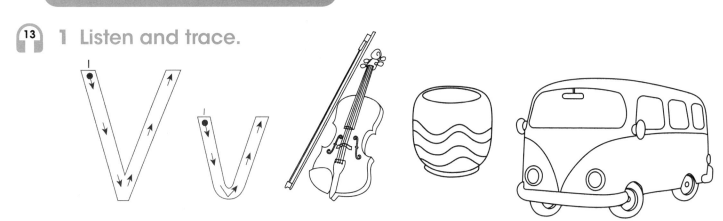

14 **2a** Listen, point and say.

15 **2b** Listen, find and say.

3 Trace and write.

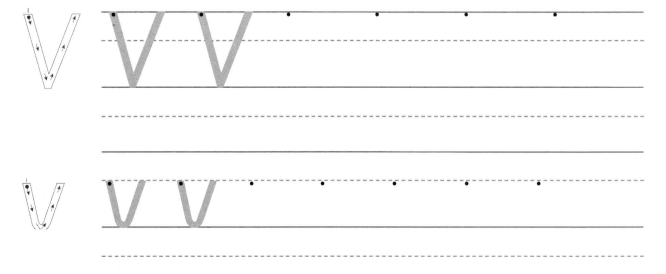

4 ▲▲ Write.

5 Complete the letter vans.
Write **V** and **v**.

V _ _ _ _

v _ _ _ _

6 Circle the things that begin with v.
Point and say.

7 ▲▲ **Read and write the missing letters.**
Then read and colour.

The boy is playing a pink _iolin.

There is a blue _ase on the table.

The girl is in the green _an.

1 Listen and trace.

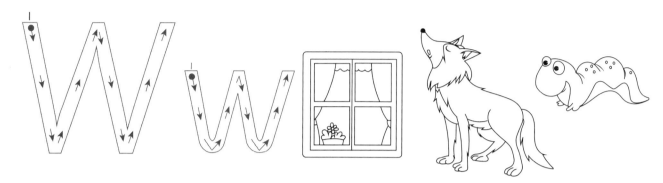

 2a Listen, point and say.

 2b Listen, find and say.

3 Trace and write.

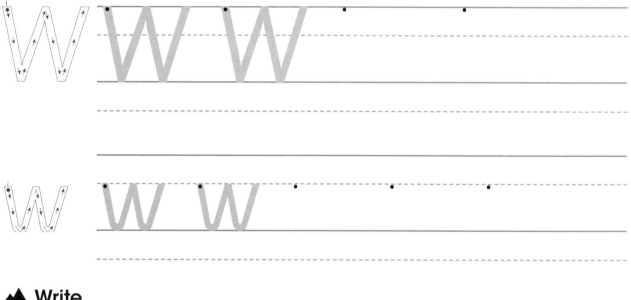

4 🔺 Write.

5 Find and trace **V, v** and **W, w.**
Use 2 colours.

u w v y v y w u v

V Y W U W V Y U V

6 Look and write **u, v** or **w.**
Then say.

_indow

_olf

_ase

_an

_mbrella

_orm

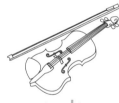

_iolin

_ncle

7 ▲▲ Say the sounds and complete the pictures.
Then write.

v + a + n   w + e + b   v + e + t

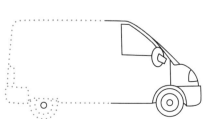
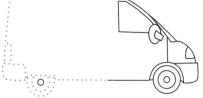

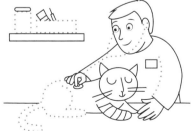

It is a _____ .   It is a _____ .   It is a _____ .

3 Let's learn our letters

 1 Listen and trace.

 2a Listen, point and say.

 2b Listen, find and say.

3 Trace and write.

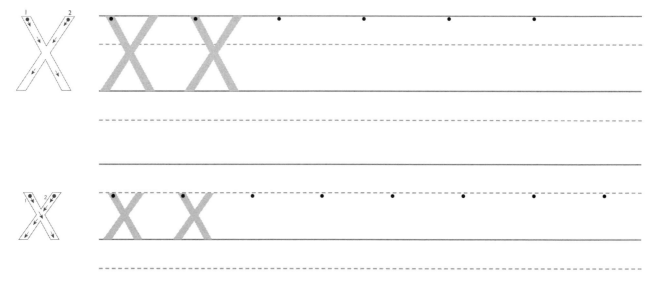

4 ⛰ Write.

5 Find and trace V, v, W, w and X, x.

Use 3 colours. Then circle and match.

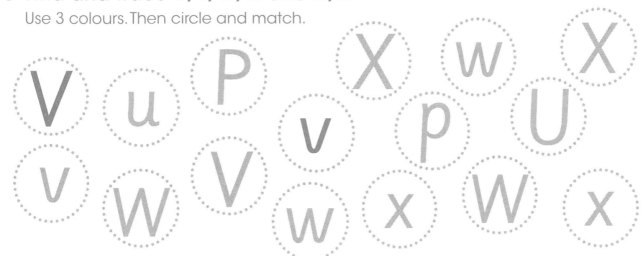

6 Look at the pictures.

Find and circle the words. Then trace the words and say.

fox

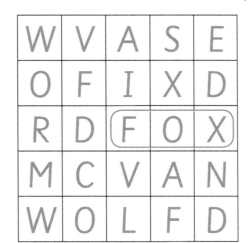

W	V	A	S	E
O	F	I	X	D
R	D	F	O	X
M	C	V	A	N
W	O	L	F	D

fix

worm

van

vase

wolf

7 ▲▲ Look and write.

 V is for _iolin.

 W is for _indow.

 X is for bo_.

4 Story time: What is in the box?

 1 Listen and point.

 2 ⇕ Listen, say and circle or write.

A van drops a box in the wood.

The wolf, worm and fox find the box.

In the box is a vase and a violin.

The fox and the worm fix the violin.

The wolf plays the violin.

The fox and the worm run away!

3 There are 3 animals in the story.
   Write the animal names.

_____

5 I can do it!

 1 Listen, find and write.

box   wolf   van   fox   vase   worm

1

The _ _ _ _ is in the _ _ _.

2

The _ _ _ and _ _ _ _ like the _ _ _ _ .

3

The boy is making a _ _ _ .

2 Draw lines to match the letters.

V   w
W   x
X   v

W   v
X   W
V   x

3 Write the missing letters.

Match the pictures that start with the same sound. Then complete.

_olf

bo_

_an

_orm

_ox

_ase

Unit 9

1 Let's learn our letters

 1 Listen and trace.

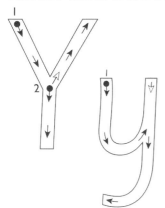

 2a Listen, point and say. Then colour.

 2b Listen, find and say.

3 Trace and write.

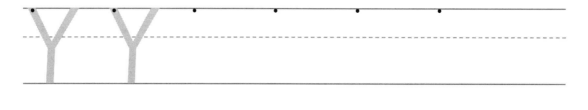

4 ▲▲ Write.

5 Complete the letter yoyos.

Write **Y** and **y**.

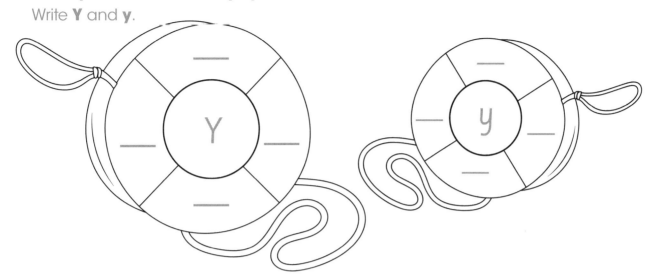

6 Find and colour the crayon.

Circle the things that begin with **y**.

7 ▲ Read and write the missing letters.

Then colour.

I can see a _ellow _o-yo.

The _ak is next to the wolf.

There is a red ladybird on the _ak.

2 Let's learn our letters

28 **1** Listen and trace.

29 **2a** Listen, point and say.

30 **2b** Listen, find and say.

3 Trace and write.

4 ▲▲ Write.

5 Find and trace **Y, y,** and **Z, z.**

Use 2 colours. Then circle and match.

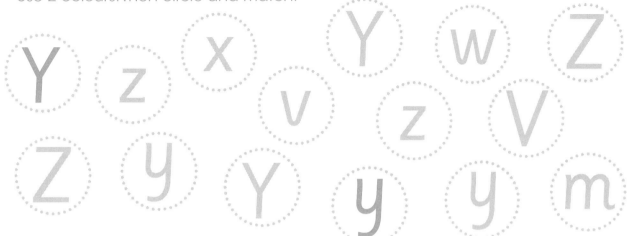

6 Look and write **x, y** or **z.**

Then say.

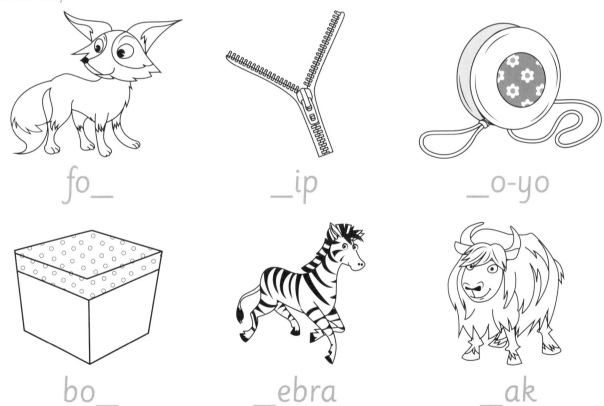

fo_   _ip   _o-yo

bo_   _ebra   _ak

7 🔺 Look and write.

 Y is for _ellow.

 Z is for _oo.

3 Let's practise our letters

1 Look and say.

Choose the right letter to complete the words.

p or b ?

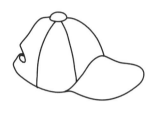

ca__

j or g ?

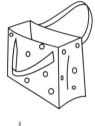

ba__

n or m ?

de__

d or p ?

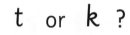

ta__

t or k ?

nu__

f or g ?

fro__

2a Make new words.

Sound them out and write.

h + a + t

__ __ __

b + e + d

__ __ __

s + i + t

__ __ __

c + o + t

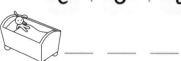

__ __ __

b + u + s

__ __ __

2b Write the middle letter from each word.

__ __ __ __ __

These letters are vowels.

3 Which words have the same letter in the middle: **a, e, i, o** or **u?**

Circle and match. Use 5 colours.

van   fix   web   bag   box   net   zip   sun   jug   fox

4 Write the words under the pictures.

_ _ _

_ _ _

_ _ _

_ _ _

_ _ _

4 Story time: Fun at the zoo

Zara and Zak are at the zoo.

Zara likes the zebras.

Zak likes the yaks.

Oh no! The zebra has got a yellow yo-yo!

Now the yo-yo is stuck on the yak.

Poor Zara! The yak doesn't like her.

3 Find the signs.

Write the missing words.

5 I can do it!

1 Listen, find and write.

Then colour.

| zebras | zoo | yak | yellow | zip | Zara | brown |

The _ _ _ is big and _ _ _ _ _.

There is a
_ _ _ _ _ _ _
_ _ _ on the
table.

_ _ _ _ loves the
_ _ _ _ _ _ in
the _ _ _.

2 Draw lines to match the letters.

Y   z

Z   y

Z
Y

y
z

3 Say the sounds to make the words.

Match to the pictures.

c + a + t

n + u + t

y + a + k

f + o + x

z + i + p

h + a + t

1 Play the game.

Listen and say the letter. Then colour the matching letter and picture.

2 Complete the alphabet.

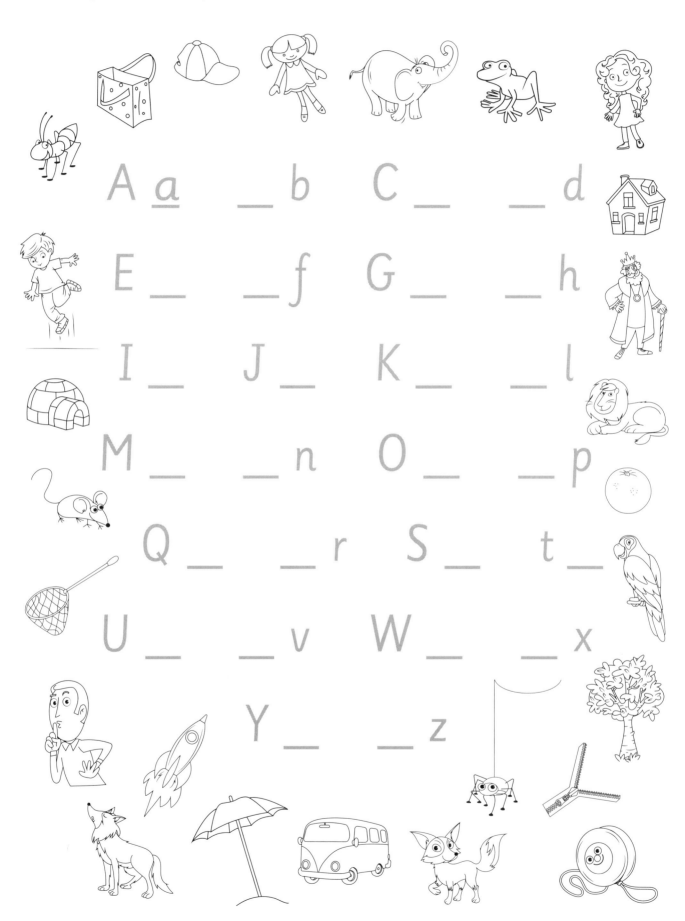

A a   _ b   C _   _ d

E _   _ f   G _   _ h

I _   J _   K _   _ l

M _   _ n   O _   _ p

Q _   _ r   S _   t _

U _   _ v   W _   _ x

Y _   _ z